Adventures in Canadian History

JANE FRANKLIN'S OBSESSION

PIERRE BERTON

JANE FRANKLIN'S OBSESSION

ILLUSTRATIONS BY PAUL MC CUSKER

An M&S Paperback Original from
McClelland & Stewart Inc.
The Canadian Publishers

An M&S Paperback Original from McClelland & Stewart Inc.

First printing January 1992

Canadian Cataloguing in Publication Data

Berton, Pierre, 1920-
Jane Franklin's obsession

(Adventures in Canadian history. Exploring the frozen world)
"An M&S paperback original."
Includes index.
ISBN 0-7710-1435-X

1. Franklin, Jane, Lady, 1792-1875 – Juvenile literature.   2. Franklin, John, Sir, 1786-1847 – Juvenile literature.   3. Northwest Passage – Juvenile literature.   4. Arctic regions – Discovery and exploration – British – Juvenile literature.   I. McCusker, Paul.   II. Title.   III. Series: Berton, Pierre, 1920-   Adventures in Canadian history. Exploring the frozen world.

G660.B47 1992   j917.19'5041'092   C91-095531-Z

Cover design by Tania Craan
Text design by Martin Gould
Cover illustration by Scott Cameron
Interior illustrations by Paul McCusker
Maps by Geoffrey Matthews; map on p. 78 adapted by James Loates
Editor: Peter Carver

Typesetting by M&S

Printed and bound in Canada

McClelland & Stewart Inc.
The Canadian Publishers
481 University Avenue
Toronto, Ontario
M5G 2E9

Contents

Adventures in Canadian History

JANE FRANKLIN'S OBSESSION

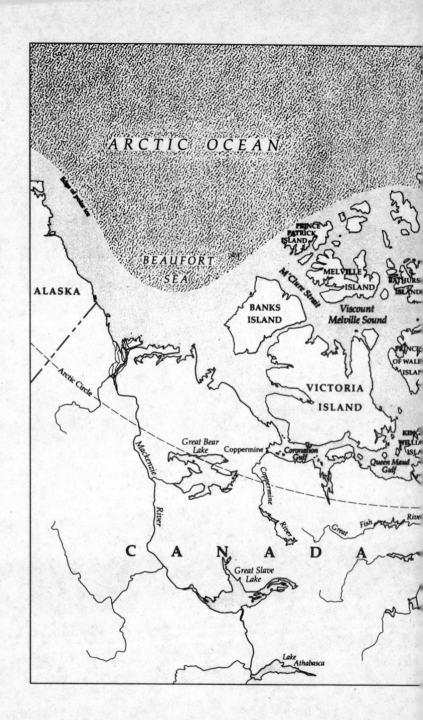

ARCTIC OCEAN

BEAUFORT
SEA

ALASKA

PRINCE
PATRICK
ISLAND

MELVILLE
ISLAND

BATHURST
ISLAND

M'Clure Strait

BANKS
ISLAND

Viscount
Melville Sound

PRINCE
OF WALES
ISLAND

Arctic Circle

VICTORIA
ISLAND

Mackenzie

Great Bear
Lake

Coppermine

Coronation
Gulf

KING
WILLIAM
ISL

Queen Maud
Gulf

Coppermine

River

River

Great

Fish

River

C A N A D A

Great Slave
Lake

Lake
Athabasca

The tireless Lady Jane Franklin with her easy-going husband, Sir John.

EVER SINCE NORTH AMERICA was discovered, seamen of all nations hoped to find a water highway, cutting through the centre of the continent of North America. They were sure it would lead on to Asia – that mysterious realm of riches: spices, silks, treasure of all kinds.

A passage through the continent would provide a short cut that would cut weeks, even months, off the regular voyage. At last they would be able to avoid the long round-about routes that led through the dreadful storms at the foot of the South American continent – Cape Horn – or the equally difficult passage at the foot of Africa – The Cape of Good Hope.

But no such easy short cut to the Orient existed. That became obvious as explorers and fur traders began to work their way across the continent and farther and farther north through Canada. If a passage did exist, it was to be found only beyond the cold mists of the Arctic.

There were some, indeed, who didn't think there could be a passage. They believed that the continent continued on north until it reached the North Pole. Others felt that there might be an ocean at the top of the continent which would be easily navigable. Others were convinced – and more rightly – that a maze of islands and wriggling channels would be found in the Arctic Ocean north of the top of North America. Perhaps these channels might form a passage that could be navigated, and the Orient reached.

From the days of Queen Elizabeth I to the twentieth century, Englishmen sought to find such a passage. One of these was a plump naval officer named John Franklin, the best known of all Arctic explorers. Much of the credit for his fame belongs to his wife, the remarkable Lady Jane Franklin. It was she who kept his memory alive after others tended to forget it.

Franklin was only one of a long line of British seamen who had vainly sought the mysterious Passage. The quest had obsessed and frustrated English sailors and explorers for almost three hundred years. As one of them, Martin Frobisher, declared, "It is *still* the only thing left undone, whereby a notable mind might be made famous and remarkable." Anybody who could find the Passage, in short, would be a hero, and a wealthy one.

Frobisher, a friend of both Drake and Hawkins, famous sea dogs who had helped defeat the Spanish Armada, was the first Englishman to seek the Passage. He made three voyages between 1576 and 1578. He was an optimistic man – a little too optimistic as it turned out. He was sure that the "strait" that he had discovered north of the Ungava

Peninsula led westward to the Pacific and that a fortune in gold lay on an island near its mouth. His backers were more interested in gold than in exploring. But the gold turned out to be "fool's gold" – iron pyrites. So Frobisher never managed to explore his strait, which we now know was only a bay on the southeast shore of Baffin Island.

Seven years after Frobisher, a more hard-headed Elizabethan sailor, John Davis, a friend of Sir Walter Raleigh, tried again. He rediscovered the great island of Greenland. Incredibly, this huge land mass had been totally forgotten after the failure of the Norse colonies three centuries before. After realizing that Greenland really *did* exist and wasn't a myth, Davis crossed the ice-choked strait that bears his name. There he charted the east coast of a new land, which we now call Baffin Island. He too was convinced the mysterious passage existed. But he couldn't get any farther north because a wall of ice barred his way.

Like Frobisher before him, Davis had noticed a broad stretch of water just north of Ungava at the tip of what is now Quebec. It was through this strait that Henry Hudson sailed in 1610; it now bears his name. Hudson burst out onto an apparently limitless sea, and thought he had reached the Pacific Ocean. He was wrong.

It was there, after a dreadful winter, that he met his death at the hands of a mutinous crew, four of whom were later murdered in a skirmish with the natives. You may have seen the famous painting of Hudson and his son being set adrift to his death in the bay that now bears his name.

Those who survived the skirmish with the natives were brought home by Hudson's first mate, Robert Bylot. That feat of seamanship was so extraordinary that he was pardoned for the mutiny. He made two more voyages to the great bay, and came to believe, rightly, that no navigable passage leading to the Pacific could be found on its western shores.

In 1616, Bylot, refusing to give up, made a fourth Arctic voyage. His pilot was a brilliant seaman named William Baffin, from whom Baffin Island takes its name. They actually got through the ice that had stopped Davis. They travelled three hundred miles (483 km) farther north than he had – a record that stood for more than two centuries.

The two seamen also mapped the entire bay that now bears Baffin's name. They found three openings in that bay, any one of which might lead to unknown lands. These deep sounds were all navigable. The time would come when they would play their part in the exploration of the frozen world. Two openings actually led to the North West Passage, and the third was the gateway to the North Pole.

After this, interest in the Passage dwindled. When Luke Foxe came home in 1631 after exploring Foxe Channel and Foxe Basin north of Hudson Bay, he insisted there could be no route to the Orient south of the Arctic Circle. That killed all hope of a commercially practical Passage.

A century later there was a brief flurry when a man named Christopher Middleton explored the west coast of the great island of Southampton in Hudson Bay. He thought he had found a channel which might lead to the

Passage, but it wasn't a channel at all, it was only a bay. He ruefully named it Repulse Bay, because it had repulsed him. Oddly enough, a century later it again became a target for those aiming at the secret of the Passage. But Repulse Bay repulsed them too.

Just as the Elizabethans had forgotten about the existence of Greenland, so the British in the early 1800's had forgotten about the whereabouts of Frobisher's discoveries. Even more astonishing, they had disputed whether there really *was* a Baffin Bay. That, in spite of the fact that whaling ships had been operating in Davis Strait for two centuries, and had undoubtedly gone into the bay. In spite of that, the bay was removed from the maps of the time.

Indeed, except for Hudson Bay and part of Baffin Island, the Arctic region was a blank on the map. Even the northern coastline of North America remained a mystery. Only two overland explorers had managed to reach the Arctic waters – Samuel Hearne, at the Coppermine's mouth in 1771, Alexander Mackenzie at the Mackenzie Delta in 1789.

But from the tip of Russian Alaska to the shores of Hudson Bay, *everything,* except for these two pinpoints, was uncharted and mysterious. And one thing was now certain: if somewhere in that fog-shrouded realm, a passage linking the oceans was found to exist, it couldn't be much more than a curiosity.

In spite of this, the British Admiralty, in the early nineteenth century, sent ship after ship into the Arctic, searching for the North West Passage. Why? The answer is that the Navy had to find something for its ships and its men and, most important, for its officers to do. For Europe was now at peace. Britain controlled the seas. The wars with France were over. The Emperor Napoleon had been packed off to exile. There were no wars left for the Royal Navy to fight. The new enemy would be the elements themselves. And so the British Navy set out to explore the world. And John Franklin was one of the explorers.

CHAPTER ONE

~

The man who wouldn't hurt a fly

JANE FRANKLIN was one of the most remarkable English women of the nineteenth century – as remarkable and as famous as Queen Victoria or Florence Nightingale.

She was known internationally and admired because, having helped to send her husband to his death in the Arctic wastes, she devoted more than ten years of her life to push the search for him. And she had a better sense than the professionals of where he might be found. She was determined to enshrine his name as one of the great Arctic heroes. In that she certainly succeeded.

Of the scores of explorers – British, American, Scandinavian, and German – who plunged into the polar wilderness, searching for the mysterious North West Passage, Franklin is by far the best known. His is the name in the school books. His is the name that springs to mind when the North West Passage is mentioned. Franklin in death succeeded where he had failed in life. The mystery of his disappearance raised him from minor Arctic hero to near sainthood. He became the symbol of nineteenth century Arctic exploration. Had he failed and survived, he would be half forgotten. Today, every schoolchild knows him – and most of the credit for that belongs to his widow.

Because of Jane's stubborn insistence that the search for Franklin and his missing crew be continued, the Arctic was opened up, its channels and islands were explored, charted, mapped, and named. When he vanished into the mists of Lancaster Sound, the world to the north of the Arctic coast-line was all but unknown. When the mystery of his fate was finally unravelled, the Arctic was no longer an unknown quantity.

Jane Franklin was thirty-six years old when she married him on December 5, 1828. Before she met John Franklin she'd turned down many suitors. Perhaps she felt that this was her last chance, though there is no evidence that she did not love and admire him. Certainly she worked hard to forward his career in the Navy.

She was not typical of her sex in an era when women spent their time at needlework or at society balls. She thirsted after wisdom: in one three-year period, she devoured 295 books. She was incurably restless and travelled a great deal. She kept a thick journal in which she noted everything in her cramped, spidery hand. At the age of nineteen, she had worked out a plan to organize her time and enrich her mind, with every moment given over to some form of study.

She was never still. She seemed to belong to everything. She was a member of the Book Society, took lectures at the

Royal Institution, visited the Newgate Prison, attended meetings of the British and Foreign School Society, and had opinions on everything.

When she met John Franklin, he was already famous as an Arctic explorer who had tried to reach the North Pole (unsuccessfully) and charted most of the Arctic coast from Alaska to the Coppermine. But Franklin's two overland expeditions to the Arctic were not without tragedy.

The first, in fact, had been a disaster. Much of it had to do with his own reckless ambition, his hunger for fame and promotion. For he had set off blindly across the barren ground of British North America without any experience.

That was in 1819 when he was thirty-three years old. He was plump, unaccustomed to hard work, and inexperienced in land travel. He'd been weak and sickly as a child – not expected to live past the age of three. He had little humour and not much imagination.

But he was certainly dogged and certainly brave – calm when danger threatened, courageous in battle. He'd gone to sea at twelve, joined the Navy at fifteen, had taken part in three of the most important battles in the Napoleonic Wars, and had been wounded badly. He had even been shipwrecked, and later rescued. He'd seen his best friend shot to death as he chatted on the deck of one of Nelson's ships, and he had survived when thirty-three out of forty officers were wounded or killed. One bombardment left him partially deaf.

He had been picked to survey the northern coast of

North America because he'd gone on a brief expedition to seek the North Pole a year or so before. That expedition had been a failure. And, in fact, there was little about that trip that could prepare him for the swift rivers of the Tundra. He had no canoeing experience, no hunting experience, no back-packing experience. But then, no other naval officer had that either.

The hard muscles required of Canadian voyageurs were looked down upon by those officers who trod the quarter-deck of a ship of the line. The Navy simply assumed its officers could do anything. It sent Franklin off to the wilds with little preparation and a minimum of equipment, and expected him and his companions to cover five thousand miles (8,050 km) by foot and canoe, and pick up what they needed from trading posts along the way. In those days, British officers did not stoop to menial tasks. All the hard work was done by the men under their command – ordinary seamen, voyageurs, and natives. This inability to share the work-load on small expeditions such as Franklin's was more than wasteful – it was dangerous. But old customs die hard, and the Royal Navy was the most rigid of the armed services.

Franklin's first North American expedition led him from Great Slave Lake to the Coppermine River, and thence to the Arctic coast. He explored the coast west as far as he could, and then headed back to Great Slave Lake again. The results, however, were disastrous. His party of twenty, including eleven voyageurs, was far too large for its hunters to feed. In spite of that, and in spite of the fact that he only had fifteen days of supplies left, Franklin, ambitious to chart as much territory as possible and perhaps find the Passage, pushed on until he was down to two bags of pemmican, and a meal of dried meat.

His paddlers were close to panic. It was clearly madness

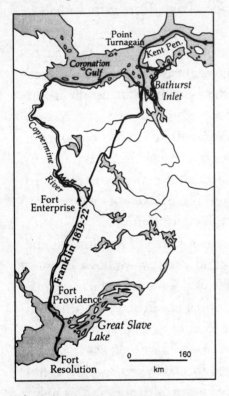

Franklin's first North American Expedition with Back and Richardson, 1819-22

to continue. Shipwreck and starvation faced them. But Franklin ignored common sense. It seemed to him that the stretch of sea-water which he had discovered at the northern tip of the continent might easily be part of the North West Passage – that it might link up with the Atlantic Ocean to the east, and the Pacific Ocean to the west. But when he reached a point called Point Turnagain, he had to give up.

He knew there wasn't a moment to lose, and yet he wasted five days on the Kent Peninsula seeking an Inuit settlement where he hoped the expedition could spend the winter. That proved impossible, and so he was forced to retreat. It was now late August, with the winter coming on. They tried to make it part of the way by ocean, but mountainous waves forced them to abandon the water route. To get back to their base on Great Slave Lake, they would have to travel overland for 320 miles (515 km).

The trip that followed was a horror. Franklin was the first to faint from lack of food – a few swallows of soup brought him around. But by mid-September the men were used to eating singed hides and a few lichens scraped from the rocks. Five days later he found he couldn't keep up.

They abandoned their canoes – a mistake, as it turned out. The Coppermine River blocked their way. How could they cross it? They were surviving on old shoes and scraps of untanned leather, enriched by the occasional meal of deer meat.

They tried to reach the river on a raft of willows. It took a week before they could cross in a makeshift canoe that they made of bits of painted canvas in which their bedding was wrapped. One of the Inuit interpreters vanished and was never seen again.

The party split into three groups. One went off to try and find Indians that could help them. The remainder split in two on October 6, when two of Franklin's voyageurs died. Another was too weak to continue and two others offered to stay with him.

Franklin and the rest stumbled on towards Fort Enterprise, their original post. Four couldn't make it and tried to move back to the previous camp. There, one of the voyageurs killed one of Franklin's officers.

Franklin himself was near death when the Indians arrived to save his life. In total he had lost eleven men from starvation and almost died in the process himself. But when he returned to England, he was a hero, known as the man who had eaten his boots. In fact his men would not have died had Franklin been more cautious and less ambitious.

One would have thought that this would be enough for Franklin, but it wasn't. He was eager to set off again in spite of his harrowing experience. But before he went he married his first wife, Eleanor Porden, a lively young poet, who, unfortunately, was suffering from tuberculosis. They were married in 1823 but they had less than twenty-three months of married life together.

Franklin was so eager to be back on another expedition to explore the Arctic coastline that he decided to leave, even though his wife was growing weaker day by day. In fact, she had drawn up her will and set her personal affairs in order. Just six days after he left, she died. He didn't get the news until he was deep in the heart of British North America.

In spite of this tragedy, he and his colleagues managed to explore a great section of the Arctic coast of North America – everything that lay between Russian Alaska, and Coronation Gulf near the Coppermine. In fact, he had opened up most of the Arctic coastline of North America, leaving a gap of only 150 miles (240 km) to be explored. Was this the route of the Passage? Franklin could not know, nor could anybody else. Twenty years would pass before he entered the Arctic again.

When he returned home, he was forty-two years old and a widower. He quickly married his wife's friend, Jane Griffin. She would soon be Lady Franklin, for a grateful government would knight her husband for his explorations.

Chapter Two
A matter of honour

ONE WONDERS WHAT Jane Franklin, who was quite the opposite of her new husband, saw in him. Perhaps it was his geniality. He was a good-hearted man, who literally wouldn't kill a fly. "The world is wide enough for both," he'd say, as he blew the insect off his hand while taking observations.

He had many friends and no enemies. Everybody liked him – liked his humility, liked his affectionate and easy nature. He was extremely religious. He read his Bible daily, prayed morning and night, and wouldn't even write a letter on Sunday.

His obvious willingness to be handled by a stronger personality must have been part of his attraction for Jane. But if her will was the stronger of the two, she was clever enough never to show it.

His mood, she noted, was easier than her own. For she saw herself as "an irritable, impatient creature" by comparison. It was her job, she said, "to combat those things that excite my more sensitive temper … to control even this disposition whenever you think it improperly excited and to exert over me ... the authority which it will be your privilege to use and my duty to yield to."

Then she added, "But do I speak of *duty?* You are of a too manly, too generous, too affectionate a disposition to like the word and God forbid I should ever be the wretched wife who obeyed her husband from a sense of duty alone." Her wedding ring, she told him, would not be "the badge of slavery, but the cherished link of the purest affection."

She was fiercely ambitious for him, and he became an extension of her own personality. She lived in her husband. When it was necessary she pushed and prodded him along in her subtle way.

She could never sit still. When, two years after their marriage, Franklin was given command of a ship in the Mediterranean, she plunged into a whirlwind of middle eastern travel through Greece, Egypt, Turkey, Syria, Asia Minor and the Holy Land by cart and carriage, by ship and canal boat, on foot and on horseback.

When he returned to England in 1833, after his service in the Mediterranean, she was in Alexandria, preparing for a trip up the Nile. That didn't stop her from directing his career by long distance. She pushed him into going to see the First Lord of the Admiralty to ask for further employment.

He was told there was nothing available, whereupon she pushed him farther. He had hoped to get a ship or a station with the Navy, but that wasn't good enough, she told him.

What he should do was go to the Arctic again. Though she didn't want him to ruin his health, she pointed out, "A freezing climate seems to have a wonderful power of bracing your nerves and making you stronger."

She badly wanted him to go after the ultimate prize – the North West Passage. In that, she did not succeed. The Navy wasn't interested.

Franklin was offered a job as Governor of Antigua, a tiny palm-fringed speck in the Caribbean. That was too much for Lady Franklin – an insulting come-down for an Arctic hero. It was a minor post, no more important than that of first-lieutenant on a ship of the line. When a better offer came, that at least *sounded* better, the Franklins accepted it. He would be Governor of Van Diemen's Land, a penal colony off the south coast of Australia.

That proved disastrous. John Franklin found himself the warden of a vast and horrible prison. In 1836 the colony consisted of more than seventeen thousand convicts and twenty-four thousand "free" citizens, many of them former convicts themselves. Each year another three thousand convicts arrived. It was a long way from the cold, clean air of the Arctic.

Franklin's six years there were the most painful of his life. He, and especially his wife, simply didn't fit in. They thought him a weakling and saw her as a meddler. She was the real problem. For she did not act the role of the ordinary governor's wife – dressing smartly, making and receiving calls, entertaining in public. Instead, she flung herself into her usual round of activity, visiting museums, prisons, and educational institutions.

That brought down a hail of criticism. She tried to look into the conditions endured by women convicts, and that didn't sit very well. She tried to start a college, but was stopped when the colonial secretary, Captain John Montague, insisted public money could not be wasted on such a project. "A more troublesome interfering woman I never saw," Montague said privately.

Instead of sitting quietly in Government House, she travelled about Australia, overland from Melbourne to Sydney by spring cart and horseback, for instance. She discussed everything, compiled statistics in her journals, and made herself unpopular.

In Van Diemen's Land they considered her the power behind the throne. Her husband was called "a man in petticoats." He was no match for the powerful and wily civil servant, Montague, who engaged in a campaign against him that could have only one ending. When Franklin fired him, Montague through his friends in the press fought back, and travelled to England to lay his case before the colonial office.

Franklin received a stinging rebuke. His wife was now in a state of nervous collapse. The newspapers reported the explorer's replacement before he himself received official notice. And so, by 1844, he had reached the bottom of his career. More important, he felt his honour had been stained – and in nineteenth century England, an Englishman's honour was all-important.

In Franklin's view, and that of his wife, there was only one way he could regain that honour, and that was to perform some magnificent feat of exploration. And so, once again, the North West Passage beckoned.

It is very doubtful if Franklin would have pushed so hard to go back to the Arctic if his reputation hadn't been at stake. He was, after all, in his sixtieth year, and that was an advanced age in which to face the Arctic blizzards. There were some who felt he was too old.

He wasn't only too old, he was also too plump. His friends worried about him if he didn't receive the posting. But others rallied to his cause. "If you don't let him go, the man will die of disappointment," was the way Sir Edward Parry, the other great Arctic explorer of his time, put it to the Navy. In short, the most ambitious Arctic expedition yet mounted by Britain was to be led by a man who got the job because everybody felt sorry for him.

When Franklin set off, the Arctic Archipelago, as it was called – a maze of islands and channels – was still largely unknown. Franklin had found the narrow channel that ran along the North American coastline between the Beaufort Sea and King William Land. A parallel channel explored by Sir Edward Parry lay three hundred miles (480 km) to the north, leading from Baffin Bay to Viscount Melville Sound.

What lay in between was a blank on the map. It was believed that a connection could be made between the two channels, and the Navy, with its usual optimism, felt it could be conquered in a single two-month season. It was Franklin's job to try to find a way between the two.

His orders were to enter the Arctic through Lancaster Sound off Baffin Bay, and to sail straight on until he reached the great ice barrier near Viscount Melville Island. When he reached Cape Walker at the entrance to Melville Sound, he was to turn south or southwest and into unknown waters to find the channel he had discovered along the Arctic coast. Having done that, he could proceed west along a fairly familiar coastline all the way to the Bering Sea.

But nobody could be sure of where he was going. There was a great blank space on the map – seventy thousand

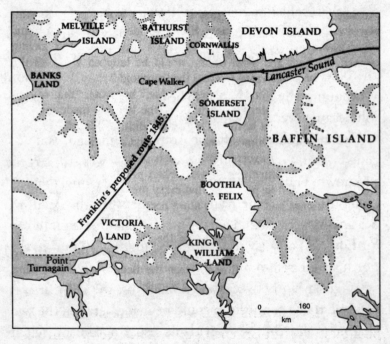

Franklin's proposed route from Cape Walker, 1845

square miles (181,370 sq km) in size – through which he had been ordered to travel. Nobody knew what it contained. It might be a vast expanse of open ocean. It might be a larger land mass. Or it might be both.

In Franklin's instructions, somebody added an afterthought. If he couldn't go through to the south, then he was given permission to try a different route, north through the unexplored Wellington Channel. That unfortunate clause in his orders would be responsible for years of useless searching in the wrong direction.

Franklin would leave on two sailing ships with twenty horsepower auxiliary engines, the first time engine power was used in the Arctic. He would have a crew of 134, and no one considered the problem of feeding them. Nobody explained why all these men were needed. The only reason was that the Navy had to keep its people busy in peacetime.

For the ordinary seaman, the voyage would often be a horror – at least in our eyes. But they were used to being crammed into tiny ships, squeezed into a swaying hammock at night, enduring back-breaking labour and wretched food by day. They faced long winters of boredom – confined to the prison of their cockle-shells, the vessels themselves covered in a mantle of snow to keep out some of the cold. Alone in the Arctic wastes, out of touch with civilization for years, unable to communicate with wives, friends, or family, and faced with the almost certain prospect of scurvy – blackened gums, loose teeth, weariness, and mental fogginess – they endured. They had joined the

Navy, not to see the world, but to provide for their families. They received double pay for Arctic exploration, and over the weary months and years, the pay mounted up.

Franklin's two ships, the *Erebus* and the *Terror*, were each larger than any previous Arctic vessel. That alone suggested difficulties in getting through some of the narrower channels, and over some of the known Arctic shallows. And incredibly, nobody had given a thought to the possibility that the expedition might encounter trouble.

Optimism reigned. Success, it was felt, was all but

certain. No plans were made for a relief expedition – it would simply have been too costly. None of the people on board were hunters. Franklin intended to exist solely on his own provisions. Apparently he dismissed the threat of scurvy. Only one of his officers had any polar background. All these deficiencies were forgotten in the wave of enthusiasm that accompanied the Franklin expedition.

The president of the Royal Geographical Society was one of the optimists. "I have the fullest confidence that everything will be done for the promotion of science, and

Franklin's two little ships leave Gravesend, May 1845, never to return.

for the honour of the British name and Navy, that human efforts can accomplish," he exalted. "The name of Franklin alone is, indeed, a national guarantee...."

And so, in the spring of 1845, the expedition set off. The two stubby little ships, gleaming in their fresh coats of black and yellow paint, were glimpsed by some Greenland whalers as they set off across Baffin Bay that summer. That was the last view the civilized world had of the *Erebus* and *Terror* and its 129 men (five were sent home sick from Greenland). None was ever seen alive again.

Chapter Three

The Great Search begins

No one knows how Franklin died, or what it was that killed him. His body was never found. Men in ships combed the Arctic for twelve years before the fate of his expedition was unravelled. For all that time, Englishmen waited in suspense.

Between 1848 and 1859, more than fifty expeditions were mounted to search for the aging explorer. Untold amounts of money were squandered. Ships sank, were lost or abandoned. Men died of mishap and scurvy. But when the great search finally came to an end, the white curtain of uncertainty had been drawn aside, the great archipelago of islands and channels had been charted, and the secret of the North West Passage – or as it turned out, *Passages* – had been unlocked. And yet a new century would dawn before anybody was able to take a ship through the Arctic from ocean to ocean.

The tale of the Franklin search is complicated and frustrating. Some of the men who took part were motivated as much by ambition as humanity. While searching for the lost ships, they were also seeking a greater prize – the elusive Passage. It needn't have taken twelve years. It didn't have to cost a sultan's ransom. It moved with maddening slowness. Franklin's fate could have been discovered as early as 1847, and some of his men could have been rescued. That didn't happen.

On the other hand, if the search hadn't taken place, the Arctic puzzle would have remained and most of that seventy thousand square mile blank space on the map might easily have been explored and claimed by some other nation with the will or the funds to conduct the probe.

Franklin's search allowed the British to claim ownership to most of the North American Arctic, which is now the Canadian Arctic. It made it possible for Canada to claim the Arctic as her own.

After two years passed with no word from Franklin, Jane Franklin began to have qualms. Returning from a whirl-wind tour of travel from the West Indies to the United States, she was dismayed by the lack of news. Everybody had confidently assumed her husband would be dispatching letters home from the Bering Strait. None came. At this point some naval men were demanding that a search party go out.

But the Navy moved with a glacial slowness. In November of 1847, with still no news from her husband and a third winter looming, she held a meeting at her home. And there she chose the explorer of the Antarctic, James Clark Ross, to lead any expedition to which the Admiralty might agree. It was clear at last that the Admiralty would agree to a search if Ross was in charge, because of his reputation.

No one except Lady Franklin was really concerned. In spite of the Admiralty's slow movement, optimism remained high. At the end of November, a local magazine interviewed a number of Arctic officers who insisted that Franklin had succeeded so well that he had already passed *through* Bering Strait and into the Pacific. But, in reality, by then Franklin had been dead nearly half a year, and his hungry crew, weakened by scurvy, were planning to abandon their ice-bound vessels.

The Great Search began in 1848. The country was beginning to show concern over the fate of the expedition. In March, the first lord of the Admiralty announced a stupendous sum – 20,000 pounds – would be paid to anybody who might help to save the lives of Franklin or his men. A later announcement offered half that sum to anyone who would merely discover what had really happened to the lost ships. That 10,000 pounds would be well over a million dollars in today's money.

The government planned an ambitious three-pronged attack that would see four ships, as well as an overland party, explore the maze of islands and channels from three directions, east, west, and south. Lady Franklin herself was tempted to join one of these. She wrote to her missing husband – one of many letters that he never received – that "it would have been a less trial to me to come after you ... but I thought of my duty & my interest to remain, for might I not have missed you … yet I've thought you to be ill, nothing should have stopped me.…"

For eighteen months, while the three search expeditions were out of touch with the world, Jane Franklin waited in hope, persisting in the belief that her husband and his companions were still alive. She sent letters with every search party. James Ross had promised her he would be back in October of 1848, with Franklin and his ships. But October came and went with no word from any of the three expeditions. November found her, in her niece's words, "much out of health & in deep despondency." And the silence continued.

In January, 1849, public prayers were being said in sixty churches for the safety of the expedition. Jane Franklin was committed heart and soul to the task of finding her missing husband. And she was employing every means to speed the search.

She went to English ports to interview whalers heading out for Baffin Bay, urging them to carry extra provisions in case they encountered the lost ships. She received a steady stream of callers in her London apartment – anybody who would tell her anything about the expedition, or make any suggestions. She even visited a mystic, who gave her the usual optimistic but inconclusive reading.

She launched into a campaign of letter writing that would have no end until the truth was known. She wrote Zachary Taylor, the new American president, appealing to his humanitarian and patriotic instincts. The president said he would do what he could.

The Admiralty, to whom she addressed another letter, was less enthusiastic. She wanted to borrow two ships and fit them out at her own expense. They refused. They sent a supply ship out after James Ross – that was enough for them. She wanted to go with it, but they refused to let her. She had to be content with another letter to her husband, who by this time had been dead for almost two years.

In the summer of 1849, she went to the Shetland and Orkney Islands in Scotland to interview more whalers who might have news of the missing men. They told her nothing. Two of the expeditions finally returned – including that of James Ross – and a kind of Arctic fever swept England. Books about polar journeys, dioramas showing Arctic vistas, newspaper and magazine articles about northern adventurers combined to increase the public interest.

But where was Franklin? Why hadn't he been found? How could two ships and 129 men vanish from sight without a word, without a hint, for almost five years? All of the expeditions returned empty-handed. Franklin seemed to have been swallowed up in the Arctic mists.

Now the Admiralty decided to send ships right around Cape Horn into the Pacific to enter the Arctic Ocean from the west. This was the first of *six* expeditions that would be sent off in 1850 to search for John Franklin.

The assumption was that Franklin had somehow got further west. There was no basis for that belief, and it didn't sit well with Jane Franklin. She resolved to fit out her own expedition. The ships would have to be small, because she couldn't afford big ones. But she was confident she could raise money in the United States. She was determined her husband be found alive or dead. "There's no trial," she declared, "that I am not prepared to go through if it become necessary."

There were vast areas in the eastern Arctic, she knew, that had not been examined. Now she determined that these too would be searched.

She decided the Navy should hire a whaling captain, William Penny. At forty-one, he was the acknowledged leader of the Davis Strait whalers. He had been in the Arctic since the age of eleven, had commanded a whaling ship for sixteen years, and knew as much about the Arctic as anybody.

Penny was certainly not the Admiralty's choice. Whalers were not naval men, and the Admiralty wanted the British Navy and not the whalers to lead the search. But Jane Franklin moved behind the scenes to confirm him in this post.

She was prepared to pay for the expedition herself, if necessary, but was able to persuade the Admiralty to come up with the funds. The idea of Franklin's lady squandering her last penny on a private quest didn't sit well with the English public, to whom she had become a heroine. The Navy gave in.

Penny carried another letter to her lost husband. "I

desire nothing," she wrote, "but to cherish the remainder of your days, however injured & broken your health may be … I live in you my dearest – I pray for you at all hours…."

At this point, May, 1850, there were ten British ships heading for the Arctic searching for Franklin. In addition there were two American naval vessels, bringing the number of search vessels to an even dozen. That too was Lady Franklin's doing. She had persuaded Henry Grinnell, a New York philanthropist and shipping merchant, to underwrite the expedition.

Yet she remained uneasy. She was no longer an amateur where the Arctic was concerned. She had seen everybody,

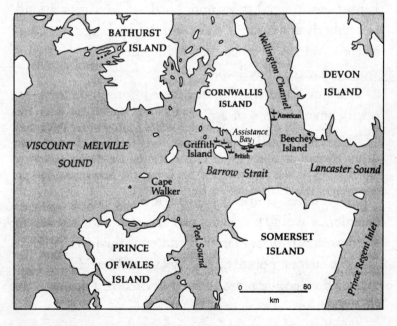

Area of the Franklin search, 1850-51

read everything, digested it all. Before the decade was out she would know more about the North than any armchair expert.

She suspected her husband's ships might have been caught on the ice – perhaps in James Ross Strait off King William Island. Perhaps they had abandoned their vessels and headed for the Great Fish River on the main continent. That was very close to what had actually happened, but Jane Franklin couldn't convince anybody of that possibility.

Expedition after expedition was setting off for the Arctic, but all were concentrating on the far North. The two American ships were heading for the very top of Baffin Bay. Penny was ordered to explore north of Lancaster Sound, but nobody apparently had considered looking at the coast to the south. And so Jane Franklin knew that she herself would have to see to that.

On June 5, her own modest expedition was ready to set off for that purpose in a ninety-ton (82 tonne) ship, the *Prince Albert,* a former pilot boat, outfitted with funds from other friends and her own dwindling fortune.

She herself drafted the orders. The commander, Lieutenant Charles Codrington Forsyth, a man with no Arctic experience, would proceed down Prince Regent Inlet to the narrowest part of Somerset Island, and then sledge south past the farthest point reached by James Ross. Had he been able to do that, he might have unlocked the riddle to the lost party.

Of all the thirteen ships searching the Arctic from the

Bering Sea to Lancaster Sound, only this one was headed in the right direction. Few seemed to remember that John Franklin was a stubborn man with a reputation for following his orders to the letter. Those letters had been explicit. He was told to head west to Cape Walker (on the northern tip of Prince of Wales Island) and then head south. Only if the ice blocked his way was he to attempt another route north through the Wellington Channel. Lady Franklin was one of the few who believed it more than possible that her husband had found a way to stick to his original instructions. But then, she knew him better than any naval friend did.

CHAPTER FOUR

~

The first clues

Of the nine ships that left England in 1850 to probe the Eastern Arctic, only one got back that year. The rest were imprisoned in the ice of Barrow Strait and Wellington Channel and, from that central point, sledging parties searching for Franklin fanned out in every direction, except the right one.

The Arctic had never seen such activity, and would not see it again in that century. At last, the mysteries of that drab and silent realm were to be unlocked.

It was in this winter that some of the explorers found the first traces of the Franklin expedition. On a tiny little islet known as Beechey Island, off Devon Island at the mouth of the Wellington Channel, they discovered his first wintering spot.

Here were three mounds supported by three weathered headboards, marking the last resting place of a trio of Franklin's seamen, who had obviously died in the winter and early spring of 1846. As the party encountered more and more relics, there was no doubt now that this had been the main camp for the two wintering ships. Here were rope

The first hint of the lost expedition: graves of three seamen who died on Beechey Island during the first winter.

fragments, sail cloth, tarpaulins, casks, clothing, blankets, and scraps of paper strewn about. Here was a small mountain of six hundred empty preserved meat tins, filled with pebbles to form some sort of ballast. There was even a pair of officer's gloves laid out to dry on a rock.

But that only deepened the mystery. Franklin had left in a hurry apparently. He'd failed to leave any kind of memorandum or paper suggesting the direction he'd taken. He might have gone anywhere. For this Gibraltar-like island stood at the crossroads of the Arctic. Channels stretched off in every direction.

Then a few hints began to appear. Sledge tracks pointed north along the east coast of Wellington Channel. These were traced for forty miles (64 km). And so it looked to the searchers as if Franklin had explored the upper waters of the channel, preparing to examine it more thoroughly when spring came. This led to the guess – a mistaken one – that he'd headed north after all.

Meanwhile, back in England, Lady Franklin was preparing to launch another expedition. Forsyth had failed to get south of Prince Regent Inlet. She determined to try again with a new captain.

William Kennedy, a tough Canadian fur trader, the son of a Cree woman and Hudson's Bay factor, volunteered even though he had never been to sea in his life. His second-in-command would be Joseph-René Bellot, a twenty-five-year-old French naval officer. He too knew nothing about the Arctic, except what he had read in books.

What they lacked in experience, this odd pair made up for in enthusiasm. Both volunteered to serve Lady Franklin's cause without fee. They came to London of their own accord and at their own expense to answer her call for help – two outsiders from alien worlds with no link to any of the several British establishments involved in the search for her husband.

Jane Franklin was by now an international heroine. She was impressed by Kennedy, who had abandoned his business and, over the protests of his family, hurried to her side. And she was stimulated by Bellot's youthful ardour. Indeed, she treated him as if he were her son.

The Admiralty wasn't so enthusiastic. The idea of a naval officer from a foreign country serving under an untutored mixed-blood from the wilds of sub-Arctic America was to them madness.

But Lady Franklin won out. After all, it was she and not the Navy who was paying for the voyage. Actually, the voyage that followed, though arduous, was one of the happiest in Arctic history.

By the fall of 1851, all but one of the ships sent to the eastern Arctic were home. Only Kennedy's was still out in the polar wilderness. Once more Jane Franklin was in despair. The discovery of John Franklin's wintering place at Beechey Island had only increased the mystery. Where on earth had he gone in the following spring of 1846? Had both vessels sunk with all hands? In all the history of Arctic exploration that had never happened. Had he been forced to change his original route? If so, why hadn't he left cairns to mark his passage?

Every effort had been made to communicate with the missing expedition. Sailors had painted or chalked gigantic messages on the cliffs. Ships had left caches of food and clothing. Foxes had been trapped and released wearing collars carrying messages in the unlikely event that some of Franklin's men might shoot them for food. Balloons were sent off with papers carrying information about the location of the rescue ships. Blue lights were flashed, guns fired, rockets exploded in the Arctic night. But the Arctic remained silent.

Apart from an unexplained scrap of British elm found by Penny off Wellington Channel, only one other clue had appeared, and it too was not identified. This was two fragments of wood that had clearly been part of a Royal Navy vessel, picked up on the south coasts of Wollaston and Victoria Land by John Rae, of the Hudson's Bay Company. Years had passed before anyone realized they were almost certainly from one of Franklin's ships.

The country grasped at straws, clinging to the belief that the lost crews might still be alive, and so did Lady Franklin. She and her friend, Sophia Cracroft, bombarded the press with anonymous letters and the Admiralty with signed petitions urging more action.

That fall, besides Kennedy in the eastern Arctic, only two other search ships remained – both in the west. And nobody knew exactly where they were. The Navy's major expeditions had been branded as a failure, and the Navy was reluctant to start any more.

There was one bright spot – public opinion was still on Jane Franklin's side. The *Times* called for a complete review of the Franklin search and insisted on knowing the government's plans for the future. It urged "a little more continuous perseverance." Her campaign was bearing fruit.

All the old Arctic hands were convinced, as were the public and press, that Franklin had gone north and vanished somewhere up the Wellington Channel. That is where everybody felt the search should continue.

In the spring of 1852, the Navy gave in to the pressure. It promised to send *five* ships this time, under a crusty old naval hand, Sir Edward Belcher. His orders were to look for the lost explorer somewhere to the north of Beechey Island. In short, in the wrong direction.

By the spring of 1852, it seemed to Lady Franklin that every corner of the Great Archipelago would be scrutinized. Nine ships were in the Arctic – one well to the north, five in the centre, two more somewhere in the west north of Alaska. And her own sloop, the *Prince Albert* under William Kennedy, was presumably searching the southern maze of channels. Everything that could be done had been done, or so it seemed. Surely before another year was out, the mystery would be solved.

Chapter Five

One final gamble

U NKNOWN TO LADY FRANKLIN, in February of 1852, Kennedy and Bellot set off on the longest sledge journey in Arctic history – 1,265 miles (2,036 km) in ninety-five days. But they had found no trace of Franklin.

They traced a great clockwise circle, down Prince Regent Inlet, across Somerset Island and Peel Sound, up to Prince of Wales Island, and north to Cape Walker. Then they moved east along Barrow Strait to Port Leopold, and back to where their ships were anchored in Batty Bay on the eastern shore of Somerset Island.

Alas, they didn't go as far south as the region of the north magnetic Pole, off King William Land, as Lady Franklin had ordered. Perhaps this was because Kennedy was suffering from snow-blindness, and perhaps also because both men thought they saw a land barrier blocking Peel Sound. Thus they assumed that Franklin could not have come that way.

It would have been more profitable if Kennedy had listened to Bellot, who wanted to go to the bottom of

Prince Regent Inlet and talk to the Inuit there. He reasoned that if more than a hundred men were lost in the area, the Inuit would at least have heard of it. He was right, but he gave in to Kennedy.

Meanwhile, at least two search vessels were missing – and seemed to be lost. These were the two ships sent out to explore the Western Arctic under Captain William Collinson and Captain Robert McClure. And so new search parties were sent out to look for the searchers.

Actually the two ships had become separated. McClure was frozen in at Mercy Bay on Banks Island, his crew close to starvation. Collinson was farther south. McClure, indeed, had discovered the North West Passage – or one of them – and was eventually rescued by some of Belcher's party who brought him overland from Mercy Bay to Beechey Island. He had, therefore, gone all the way from west to east – but not entirely by ship. Much of the journey had been made by sledge, and so although the Passage had been discovered, it had not yet been navigated.

As for Belcher's five-ship expedition, it ended in total confusion. To everybody's astonishment and disgust, Belcher actually abandoned four ships in the Arctic, all in good condition, and none in any real danger of being trapped for a second winter.

An aging and cranky commander, he had no intention of spending another season in the Arctic, and so committed the worst blunder of the entire search. This "last of the Arctic voyages," as Belcher was to call it, was also, apart from the Franklin loss, the most disastrous. The mystery had not been solved. Captain Collinson and his missing vessel had been callously forsaken, and four big naval ships, all in perfect condition, abandoned. Sir Edward Belcher became the laughing stock of the Royal Navy.

On January 12, 1854, Jane Franklin got the first of several shocks. The Admiralty, without waiting for Belcher or any others to return, announced that as of March 31, the names of all the officers and crew member of the *Erebus* and *Terror* would be struck from its books.

She was stunned. She already had the first news of McClure's discovery of the North West Passage. Was that all that counted? Her husband's fate was still unknown. There were a few who held out the hope he or some of his crew were still alive among the Inuit. She was one of these, but now it seemed as if the long quest for the Arctic hero had been a sham – an excuse to seek not human beings, but the elusive Passage.

She wrote an indignant letter to the Admiralty. She called the Navy's decision "presumptuous in the sight of God." In a bold act of defiance, she refused to wear black mourning, and appeared in brilliant pink and green. That was to show she hadn't given up hope.

Four days before her husband was officially declared dead, the Crimean War broke out between Russia on one side and Turkey, England and France on the other. The Navy couldn't afford the luxury of any more Arctic searches. Every ship would be needed in the struggle against the Russians.

With Belcher's return in the late fall, the Admiralty lost all stomach for polar exploration. In just two years, six ships had been abandoned, or lost. Why waste any more money on a wild goose chase? Jane Franklin could argue that the fate of her husband and crew were still unknown. But even that point was lost when the Hudson's Bay's explorer, John Rae, arrived in England with the first firm news.

At Pelly Bay, on April 21, 1854, an Inuit told a fascinating tale – one that would be worth 10,000 pounds to Rae and his men. He'd heard stories from other natives of thirty-five or forty whites who had starved to death some years before, west of a large river, perhaps ten or twelve days' journey away. Later, the natives brought a treasure trove of relics to him, easily identified as having belonged to Franklin and his men – silver forks and spoons, marked with officers' crests, one of Franklin's medals, a small plate bearing his name, and other relics, including a gold watch, a surgeon's knife, and a silver pencil case.

When Lady Franklin learned, in the spring of 1856, that Rae had succeeded in his claim for the 10,000-pound reward offered for finding some clues to her husband's fate, she was irritated and dismayed. It was far too early, she said, to come to any conclusion as to what had happened. Rae's prize might confirm the government's belief that her husband was dead, but she couldn't bring herself to accept that.

She attacked the Admiralty again, "though it is my humble hope and fervent prayer that the Government of my country will themselves complete the work they have done and not leave it to a weak and helpless woman to

The Inuit bring relics of the lost expedition to John Rae.

attempt the doing that imperfectly which they themselves can do so easily and well, yet, if need be, such is my painful resolve, God helping me."

Of course, she was anything but weak and helpless. She was iron-willed and had the support of some of the most powerful figures in the country, not the least of whom was Prince Albert, the husband of the queen. She was a formidable public figure, having captured the imagination and appealed to the chivalry of the ordinary Briton, who saw her, indeed, as a weak and helpless woman, battling for her husband's life and honour. Almost single-handedly she had created a myth, turning John Franklin, a likeable, but quite ordinary naval officer, into *the* Arctic hero.

No explorer was ever as obsessed as Jane Franklin. She could not let go. Her obsession sustained her, giving her life a meaning and a focus. Her Pall Mall residence in London was nicknamed The Battery, because she had battered the Admiralty with so many letters and memorials. And when she wasn't battering against the walls of officialdom, or writing to foreign powers, or penning letters to the *Times,* thinly disguised under false names, she was influencing events from behind the scenes.

It was Lady Franklin who persuaded thirty-six of London's leading men of science, including all the major Arctic explorers, to send a memorial to the prime minister, suggesting that some of Franklin's men were still alive among the Inuit, and urging further action.

She kept up the public barrage the following year, while her allies worked for her in Parliament. She had appealed to the prime minister the previous December, and now that lengthy letter, which ran to more than three thousand words, was circulated in pamphlet form. It announced she was prepared to sacrifice her entire available fortune to pay the cost of a private expedition, if the government didn't budge.

At the same time she managed to arrange for a group of Americans to back her case with the Admiralty. It had little effect. But she would not be stopped. She had her eye on a steam yacht in Aberdeen, the *Fox*. She bought it for two thousand pounds and persuaded an old Arctic hand, Leopold M'Clintock, to take it to the Arctic to King William Island – the one spot that nobody had yet searched. There, she was certain, the secret of her husband's fate would be unravelled.

The Admiralty offered some help in the form of provisions. And M'Clintock offered to captain the ship at no cost to Lady Franklin. This was a small schooner-rigged steam yacht of 170 tons (154 tonnes), half the size of one of Franklin's vessels.

It had only made one voyage – to Norway. The quarters for the ship's company of twenty-five (seventeen of whom had taken part in previous Franklin searches) were incredibly cramped. The officers were "crammed into pigeon holes" to make room for provisions and stores. The room in which five persons ate was only eight feet (2.4 m) square. A few small coal stoves replaced the standard heating apparatus.

But to M'Clintock, who had been moved by the wave of

public sympathy that swept the country when his expedition was announced, confirmed the impression that "the glorious mission entrusted to me was in reality, *a great national duty.*"

He refused to take a single penny from Lady Franklin. The other commissioned officers followed suit. Allen Young, his sailing master, not only served without pay, but also donated five hundred pounds to the public subscription that was rapidly approaching the three-thousand-pound mark. All the same, Jane Franklin would still have to dip into her own funds for an additional seven thousand.

And so, on the last day of June, 1847, before the ship sailed from the Orkneys for Greenland, she came down to Aberdeen to bid him goodbye. He could see how deeply agitated she was when she left the yacht. He tried without success to prevent the crew from giving her the usual three lusty cheers. Public demonstrations of that kind embarrassed her. They cheered anyway, and for that, M'Clintock was grateful.

And so the *Fox* set off on the last expedition to search for John Franklin. Twelve years had gone by since Franklin set out to find the Passage. And now the final voyage of that long search to discover his fate had been dispatched.

CHAPTER SIX

The cruise of the Fox

T HE FOX HEADED out into the Atlantic. At this point M'Clintock read to the crew a letter Lady Franklin had given him before he left, reminding him that the expedition had three purposes. These were: first, and most important, the rescue of the survivors; second, the recovery of "the unspeakably precious documents of the expedition"; and third, the proof of her own claims, that "these martyrs in a noble cause achieved at their last extremity" the discovery of the North West Passage.

"My only fear," Jane Franklin wrote, "is that you may spend yourselves too much in the effort; and you must therefore let me tell you how much dearer to me even than any of them is the preservation of the valuable lives of the little band of heroes who are your companions and followers."

And so, the final voyage had begun. "I am doomed to trial & to struggle on to the end," Jane Franklin had written a year before. That struggle was continuing. But at last the end was in sight.

That was her triumph. This remarkable Victorian

gentlewoman had inspired a loyalty that queens might envy and, through her persistence, added a footnote to history. As one newspaper wrote, "What the nation would not do, a woman did."

The *Fox* reached Upernavik on the western coast of Greenland on August 6, 1857. M'Clintock had hoped to push westward, straight to the main ice-pack in Baffin Bay, but the ice was too much for him. His only chance was to try to get around it by heading north and circling before coming south again. To do that he would have to cut directly across the shallow crescent of Melville Bay. That was the most feared stretch of open water on the Greenland coast. To his dismay, he found that conditions there were the worst on record.

He managed to push his ship three-quarters of the way across, before he was blocked. But M'Clintock never lost his cool. If his ship was trapped in ice, well then, he would wait until the next year and do it again.

Yet he had to be concerned. The crew did not know what was going on. But he did. He was faced with eight lonely winter months trapped in the ice pack.

That was bad enough. The danger of being crushed was worse. The *Fox* wasn't powerful enough to push the ice floes apart. All attempts to blast it free failed. By September he'd lost control of his ship. He decided to make the best of it.

He organized a school, unpacked an organ, and taught his men to build snow houses on the ice. Two Inuit hunters in the party brought in seals and an occasional bear. Meanwhile, the ice pushed the ship farther and farther south –

farther and farther away from their goal. By April 26, they had been caught on the ice for 250 days and they had travelled 1,385 miles (2,230 km), most of it in the wrong direction.

The ice began to break, and a scene of terror followed. The ship rolled wickedly in the heavy seas, bruised and buffeted by the ice floes. M'Clintock knew that a single blow by one of those monster ice blocks could crush his ship in an instant. At times the *Fox* shuddered so violently that ship's bells rang and crewmen were almost knocked off their feet.

"Such a battering … I hope not to see again," M'Clintock wrote, describing one eighteen-hour period of torment. He knew then, he said, why a man's hair could turn grey in a few hours.

Then suddenly it was over. The ice was gone. They were free. M'Clintock could have gone south into harbour at St. John's, Newfoundland, to repair his ship and take on extra food. He didn't. Instead he went right back up the coast of Greenland and across Melville Bay, fighting his way once again through the ice.

Finally he reached the mouth of Lancaster Sound – the only real entrance into the Arctic maze. He used up most of his coal fighting his way through the ice, but he found more in a depot that Belcher had left at Beechey Island, Franklin's first wintering place. And from that point the real voyage began.

M'Clintock realized that Franklin must have gone south

down Peel Sound to the west of Somerset, in spite of what the early explorers had said about the ice barring the way. That was the only route that hadn't been thoroughly explored. He could see Cape Walker in the distance at the northern tip of Prince of Wales Island. Franklin had been ordered to go south of the Cape. And so M'Clintock followed in his track, "in a wild state of excitement – a mingling of anxious hopes and fears!"

After twenty-five miles, a dike of ice barred his way.

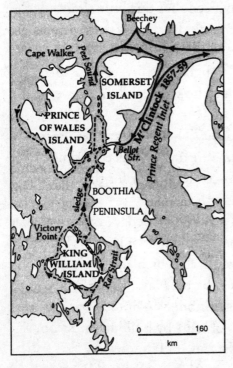

M'Clintock's expedition to King William Island, 1857-59

There wasn't a moment to lose. He turned about and chose another route.

He decided to go down Prince Regent Inlet and then try to slip back in to Peel Sound by way of a narrow passage named for Bellot. He pushed the *Fox* westward through Bellot Strait and was halfway through before he knew it. Now all he had to do was wait at the mouth of the strait until the ice vanished. He had no choice anyway. A stiff current drove the *Fox* helplessly back "almost capsizing it."

M'Clintock was convinced that this little strait was the link to the North West Passage. It was only twenty miles (32 km) long and scarcely a mile (1.6 km) wide at its narrowest point. Once they were through it, they were in easy reach of King William Island, which he knew held the answer to the Franklin mystery.

But this was not to be. They tried six times to get through Bellot Strait and were driven back each time by the ice. And so they were forced to anchor for the winter in a sheltering inlet at the eastern end.

M'Clintock planned three major sledge expeditions that winter. And this time they would use some dogs. This most efficient form of Arctic travel, which the Inuit had long known, had been rejected by the Navy, which preferred to put men in harness. In addition, M'Clintock was prepared to save the extra weight of tents by building snow houses. He was learning from the Inuit at last.

On a scouting trip, down the west coast of Boothia Peninsula, he encountered a group of four Inuit. These were

M'Clintock teaches his men to build snow houses.

the first natives they had run into. M'Clintock noticed that one was wearing a naval button. They told him it had come from some white men who had starved on an island and a river. One of the Inuit had been to the island and brought back some wood and iron.

M'Clintock offered to trade presents for information and relics. A day or so later, an entire village of forty-five arrived – men, women, and children. M'Clintock was able to bring to the *Fox* a quantity of silver cutlery, a medal, part of a gold chain, several buttons, and knives, fashioned by the natives out of wood and iron, obviously from the wrecked ship.

But none had seen any of Franklin's lost crew. One had seen the bones of a white man, who'd died on an island in the river many years before – probably Montreal Island in the delta of the Great Fish River on the main coast of North America. One or two remembered a ship crushed by the ice, to the west of King William Island. They said the vessel had sunk, but the crew had got off safely. Thus the vague outlines of the Franklin tragedy began to emerge.

M'Clintock set off again south on April 2. He met more Inuit that told him of two ships – one had sunk, the other had been forced ashore badly damaged. White men had been seen, they told him, hauling boats south toward a large river on the mainland.

Then, on a frozen channel between Boothia Peninsula and King William Island, M'Clintock came upon a village whose inhabitants had more Franklin relics, including a silver plate, bearing the crests of the explorer and his first officer, and other members of the expedition.

There were more hints of the lost party: tales of the wreck of a ship without masts, of books strewn across the Arctic wastes, of white men who dropped in their tracks on the way to the Great Fish River, some of whom were buried, and some not.

M'Clintock met an old woman and a boy who'd been the last to visit the wrecked ship, apparently during the winter of 1857-58. But the dates were vague and much of the information second-hand.

M'Clintock moved south along the island's eastern coastline and encountered more Inuit. In that treeless land, wood was more precious than gold. They'd made kayak paddles, snow shovels, spear handles, tent poles, and a variety of objects from wood they'd got from other Inuit. Obviously it had been scavenged from a ship, but none of these people knew anything about white men who had died on their shores.

M'Clintock knew his task would not be easy. The natives had plundered everything they could find, throwing away what they didn't need – such as books and papers – adapting the rest for their own use. And a ghostly shroud of snow still covered the land, hiding the remains of the lost men.

It was all very frustrating. M'Clintock kept on south to Montreal Island on the Great Fish Delta, haunted by the shades of men long dead. Here, he and his party found a bit of a preserved meat tin, and some scraps of iron and copper. These too were second-hand relics. A native stone marker made it clear that this was plunder taken earlier and set aside for later. In the eerie silence of the Arctic spring, M'Clintock circled the bleak and rugged coastline of Montreal Island by dog team. But he found no evidence that any of Franklin's crew had got that far.

He turned back on May 24 to King William Island, travelling along the sea ice that overlapped the shore. Driving his own team, he kept a sharp lookout. Again, snow shrouded the beach. At midnight, with the sun still bright in the sky, he trudged along a gravel ridge that had been swept clean, and there, with dramatic suddenness, he came upon a human skeleton.

This was a major find – the only first-hand evidence anybody had yet had of the Franklin disaster. There it lay, a grisly witness to history, the body face down, as if the owner had stumbled forward and dropped, never to move again. The bones were as white as chalk. A few rags clung to them. The limbs bore signs of having been gnawed at by animals.

He'd been a young man, slight, probably a steward, or an officer's servant. He hadn't been warmly clad. A clothes brush and a pocket comb lay close by. Gazing down on his grim find, M'Clintock remembered what an old Inuit woman had said to him: "They fell down and died as they walked along."

Up the gloomy and desolate west coast of the island, M'Clintock's party moved. He was sure that Franklin's men must have left some sort of record. But if they had, the Inuit had scattered it to the winds. If only the Navy had been quicker in its rescue operations, if the old Arctic hands hadn't been so short-sighted, if Lady Franklin's own ships had only kept going, the full story of Franklin's fate would undoubtedly have been discovered. At this late date, finding it seemed hopeless.

And then, farther up the coast, he came upon a cairn, built by another of his sledging parties, containing a message. One of his lieutenants, William Hobson, had been there six days before. He had seen nothing of a wrecked ship. He'd met no natives. But he *had* found a document! In a cairn at Victory Point on the northwestern shore of King William Island, he discovered the only record ever found of the lost Franklin expedition. It wasn't much, but it was enough to clear up the main points of the mystery.

THE DOCUMENT FOUND at Victory Point provided the only first-hand information ever uncovered about the progress and fate of the missing crews. Actually, there were two messages – two cramped scribbles written a year apart in the margins of a regular Admiralty form.

The first message was dated May 28, 1847, and was signed by Lieutenant G. M. Gore. It was cheerful enough: "All well," it read. It revealed that Franklin had certainly gone up the Wellington Channel and had, in fact, circled round before settling down at Beechey Island for the winter of 1845-46.

It also revealed that he had been caught on the ice stream just west of the northern tip of King William Island during his second winter in the Arctic. Gore and his party of seven were fully confident the two ships would be freed that summer and the Passage discovered.

But that was wishful thinking as the second message made clear. Written in a different hand and signed by Franklin's two deputies, Lieutenant Francis Crozier, and

Lieutenant James Fitzjames, it was dated April 27, 1848, and told a gloomier story.

Franklin had died the previous June, only a month after Gore had scribbled his first message. At the time of the second message, the ships had been trapped on the ice for nineteen months. No fewer than nine officers (including Gore) and fifteen men were dead. The rest had left the two vessels and were trying to reach the Great Fish River. Now there was enough to piece together the probable story of the last expedition of Sir John Franklin.

Racing to make time before the onset of autumn weather in 1845, Franklin apparently didn't stop to build cairns or leave letters. With sails full out, he pressed confidently on to the open waters of Lancaster Sound. After all, the eternal optimist expected to be sailing into the North Pacific in less than a year – why leave a message?

He pushed on through Barrow Strait. Somewhere ahead loomed the cliffs of Cape Walker, the last known point of land. To the southwest lay the Unknown, which his instructions had ordered him to explore.

But he found that direction blocked by ice. On the western shore of Devon Island he could see a stretch of clear water – Wellington Channel. And so, following his instructions, he made for this alternate route and sailed north into unexplored territory. Was it a strait, or merely a bay? No map could tell him.

The two ships headed north until the presence of an unnamed and unexplored peninsula (now the Grinnell

Peninsula) forced them to the northwest. At the very tip of the peninsula, Franklin once again found his way barred by a wall of ice.

He was forced to go back south through a different channel. Now he realized he'd rounded Cornwallis Land, which was actually an island. He went back into Barrow Strait north of Cape Walker and was again frustrated in his attempt to push west. But directly to the south he found another channel, and he knew that beyond that, some-

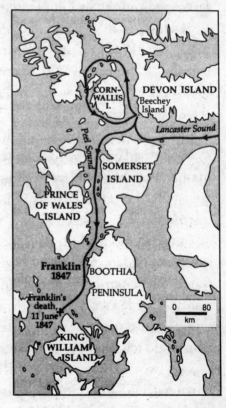

Franklin's last expedition, 1845-47

where in the area of King William Land, the way was clear to the western sea. Earlier explorers had discovered that.

It was obviously too late to make the attempt that year. He'd have to find a safe anchorage. And so he made for Beechey Island and spent the winter there, where three of his men died of natural causes – not an unusual number – and were buried on the spot. (Almost 150 years later, these bodies were exhumed, and it was discovered that the men had died from a combination of tuberculosis and perhaps lead poisoning).

Now he was within 350 miles (563 km) of his goal. Once the gap between Beechey Island and King William Land was closed, he would be near familiar waters leading west. Why didn't he leave a note for others to find? He spent the entire winter there. He was equipped for the usual activities – amateur theatricals, target practice, scientific observations, the collection of specimens. Yet no one, apparently, thought to leave a single scrap of paper outlining the expedition's plans for the following summer.

That is the mystery surrounding the tragedy. It raises questions that cannot be answered. Was it because the optimistic explorer was so certain of getting through that he really didn't think it necessary? Was it because the two ships were driven away from Beechey along the ice in a sudden spring gale, before he had time to prepare a record? Or did he actually leave a message that was never found? No one knows.

What is known is that he followed orders and set his course that spring for the south. He didn't realize he was sailing directly toward the great ice stream that pours down from the Beaufort Sea. Driven by the winds from the northwest, this mighty frozen river, frightening in its power, squeezes its way between the bleak islands, as it seeks warmer waters. It is like a floating glacier, up to one hundred feet (30 m) thick, unbroken by any channel. It forms a slow moving wall of ice that nobody can penetrate.

Flowing down between Melville and Banks Islands and through Melville Sound, the ice stream forces itself against the western shores of Prince of Wales Island. Then it curves down the unexplored channel on the eastern side of Victoria Land to block the narrows at King William Land. There its southern edge encounters the warmer waters flowing from the continental rivers and begins to break apart, leaving the channels to the south fairly clear.

Faced with the presence of this vast, slow moving frozen mass, Franklin had to turn back. But another unknown channel, Peel Sound, lay to the south. It too beckoned in the direction of King William Land. He turned his ships south into these mysterious waters. It seemed to be clear because he was sheltered from the ice stream by the bulk of Prince of Wales Island.

When he emerged from Peel Sound he would have seen the northern tip of King William Land dead ahead – only a hundred miles (160 km) away. But once he emerged from the protecting shield of Prince of Wales Island he would again have encountered the ice stream. To stay clear of that he'd have to cling to the west coast of Boothia Peninsula.

But sooner or later he knew he would be forced to face the ice, because the only route to the known Passage shown on the maps led directly down the west coast of King William Land.

In 1846, Franklin had no way of knowing that King William Land was an island. He could have got away from the ice stream by cutting around the island's eastern side and slipping down the narrow strait that separates it from the main coast of North America. But Franklin would have thought this was a dead end, since he believed King William Land was a peninsula.

And so he turned his ships into the ice stream and winter closed in. On September 12, 1846, the *Erebus* and the *Terror* were imprisoned in the frozen river that moved south at the agonizingly slow speed of one and one-half (2.4 km) miles a month.

The explorer died the following June. The mystery of his death has never been found, nor has his burial place. He was almost certainly buried at sea, but we don't know what caused his sudden passing. All was well when Gore scribbled that first message. A year later, as a second message made clear, Franklin was gone and Lieutenant Crozier was in command. All we know is that Franklin was not healthy and was in his sixtieth year. He was obviously too old to undertake such a quest – the victim of his friends' sentiment, the Navy's rigidity, and his own optimism and his wife's ambition.

The fate of his men is less mysterious. Over the years

more skeletons and fragments of skeletons have been discovered. Modern research has shown evidence of cannibalism, scurvy, and lead poisoning from the poorly soldered tins of meat. The Inuit description of the crews' final stages suggests that most died from scurvy – the disease that haunted almost every Arctic expedition. Scurvy can be cured by fresh vegetables, fresh fruits, and also fresh meat, as the Inuit well knew. But the two Franklin ships were heavily stocked with salt meat. That contributed to their fate.

The story was a familiar one, as the messages at Victory Point suggested. All was well one year; twenty-four men were dead the next. And with the men dying daily in the following winter, Crozier knew his only hope lay in abandoning the ship before the entire company perished.

For the *Erebus* and the *Terror*, there was no way out of the floating trap. It had been the coldest winter in living memory. The ice hadn't melted. Its progress was too slow.

Crozier's mistake was to head south to the Great Fish River. Perhaps he thought that a relief party might have been sent there. If so, he underestimated the slowness of the British Admiralty, and the foolish optimism of the Arctic Council of Polar Experts, who showed little concern about Franklin, and didn't move until the spring of 1848, when the surviving crews were already sledging to their deaths.

It would have been impossible for Crozier's weakened men to navigate the many cataracts of the Great Fish River even if they'd reached it. Up the coast of Prince Regent

Sound lay a cache of goods and provisions dumped there by a previous expedition. But it's doubtful if they could have reached that either, since they neither had dogs or dog drivers, and the sledges were too heavy and cumbersome to move swiftly.

M'Clintock came upon one of these Navy sledges not far beyond the rugged cape he named for Captain Crozier. What he saw shocked him. The sledge itself was a monstrous contraption of iron and oak, weighing at least 650 pounds (295 kg). On top of it was a twenty-eight foot (8.5 m) boat rigged for river travel weighing another seven or eight hundred pounds (317-362 kg). To M'Clintock, this was madness. Seven healthy men would have had trouble hauling it any distance, even if it hadn't been loaded.

But it *was* loaded – with an incredible stock of useless articles. Here were books, every kind of footgear, towels and toothbrushes, gun covers and twine, soap and sheet lead, dinner knives, crested silver plate, pocket watches and tools, a bead purse, a cigar case – everything, in short, that the civilized traveller considered necessary for his comfort and well being. But as M'Clintock wrote, it was for a sledge traveller of those times "a mere accumulation of dead weight … "

Inside he found eerie evidence of this truth. Here were sprawled two skeletons – one of a slight young man, the other of an older and sturdier seaman. They'd got this far and no farther. While their comrades had abandoned most of their supplies and struggled on, they had been left behind.

M'Clintock was convinced they were returning to the ship for more provisions. But the ship was at least sixty-five miles (105 km) to the north. Unable to drag their boat further, they'd left the two weakest of their number with a little food, some tea and chocolate, expecting perhaps to return with fresh stock. Scurvy, which weakens the muscles, also clouds the mind, making its victims believe they can accomplish more than they are able to.

At Victory Point where the cairn containing the message

was found, there was another extraordinary pile of goods. This was further proof that the men who abandoned the ships weren't aware of the extent to which they had been weakened. They piled their sledges with ten tons (nine tonnes) of gear and abandoned most of it three days later when they reached Victory Point.

The huge heap of discarded woollen clothing was four feet (1.3 m) high. But they'd also brought along button polish, heavy cookstoves, brass curtain rods, a lightning conductor, and a library of religious books. Why? It had taken them three days to haul this enormous quantity of useless

M'Clintock comes across the skeletons of two of Franklin's crew.

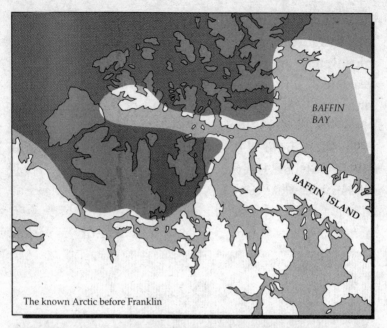

The known Arctic before Franklin

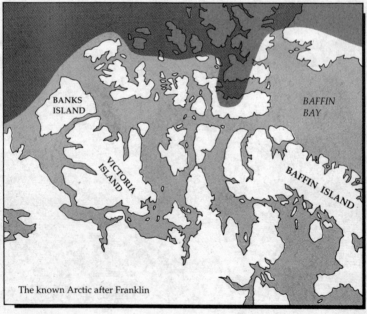

The known Arctic after Franklin

articles fifteen miles (24 km), before they realized they couldn't go farther. And so, after thawing out some ink and scribbling the second note, they lightened their sledges and headed south to their deaths.

M'Clintock left this gloomy scene on June 2, and was back on the *Fox* on June 19. No other trace of Franklin had been found, except on King William Island. But together, three sledge expeditions from the *Fox* had charted eight hundred miles (1,287 km) of new coastline. So that, by now, almost all that part of Arctic Archipelago had been unveiled as a result of the long, blundering search for Franklin.

That was a supreme irony of the quest for the North West Passage. The Passage itself would have little commercial value, even with the development of modern ice breakers. It was a symbol to gain public support for geographical and scientific investigation. And a symbol it remained.

Had Franklin been able to make his way through it, further exploration would have been postponed, probably for decades. The continued bungling of the Navy kept the flame alive and prolonged the explorations, and that was partially due to Lady Franklin's continual campaign. It had cost a great deal of money and taken a long time and caused the deaths of several men, but it wasn't entirely wasted. By the time M'Clintock returned to England, in September of 1859, most of the southern Arctic had been mapped.

M'Clintock meets with Lady Franklin.

CHAPTER EIGHT

∼
The sainthood of John Franklin

L ADY FRANKLIN WAITED restlessly for M'Clintock's
return. But she could not stay still. So off she went,
with her niece Sophia, on another of those exhausting journeys that marked her career. She said she did it to
strengthen herself for the possible solution of the long
drama, which she hoped M'Clintock would unveil.

What if he failed? How much longer could she continue
the struggle to reclaim her husband's honour? How many
more expeditions might be needed? And how many more
could she afford to finance? There was so little time.

On her sixtieth birthday she had scribbled: "I cannot
write down all the feelings that press upon me now as I
think how fast the sands of life are ebbing away." But this
was premature. In 1858, six years after she wrote those
words, while M'Clintock was enduring the freeze up in Bellot Strait, she determined to set off once more. She wouldn't
go on foot this time because she was suffering from phle-
bitis. She would travel by boat and train through France,
Greece, the Crimean battlefields, and North Africa.

Everybody knew her; everybody met her. In Athens she had an audience with the Queen of Greece, in Tunis with the Bey himself and his prime minister in the privacy of his harem, which, out of feminine curiosity, she asked to see.

She had not returned to London when M'Clintock arrived. She was on a mountain top in the Pyrenees, having been sent there for her health and carried to the peak by porters. The news reached her in a terse telegram relayed by the British consul at Bayonne, who'd received an equally terse letter from M'Clintock. This gave her the details of his findings and added, almost as an afterthought, that her husband could not have suffered long and had died with success in sight.

She hurried back to London to find herself the most admired woman in the realm. She had triumphed where the Navy had failed. Persistently, year after year, she had pointed in the right direction, secure in the belief that her husband, a stickler for orders, would follow his instructions to the letter, even at the risk of his life.

He'd been told to go south, and south he'd gone. All along she had known he would. The relics of the expedition went on display at the United Services Institution, where the crowds were so thick it was necessary to issue tickets. The press was urging that Parliament reimburse her for the funds she had spent on the search. She replied she wouldn't accept a penny. But she did want to do something for M'Clintock and his crew. And she also wanted to do something more for her husband. She was determined that he, and not McClure, should be recognized as the man who first solved the puzzle of the Passage.

There were honours aplenty for the crew of the *Fox*. They were all granted the Arctic Medal. The officers were promoted. M'Clintock was toasted and honoured – with the freedom of the City of London, with honorary degrees from three leading universities in Britain, with a fellowship and a medal from the Royal Geographical Society, and a knighthood from the queen.

In March, 1860, Lady Franklin, working behind the scenes as usual, prompted a debate in Parliament that resulted in an award of 5,000 pounds to the crew of the *Fox*. Of that M'Clintock received 1,500.

She herself was awarded the Patron's Medal of the Royal Geographical Society, becoming the first woman ever to receive that honour. With that went the prize she had sought for her husband – a memorial from the Royal Geographical Society, testifying to the fact that his expedition had indeed been the first to discover a North West Passage.

That made it clear there was no single channel to the Arctic, but several. Whether Franklin had actually seen the last link of the Passage, before he died so mysteriously, was never argued. Obviously he hadn't. He must have been aware, of course, that the channel in which his ships were trapped led inevitably to the Pacific along the coastline of North America. But to call him the discoverer of the Passage was stretching the known facts.

That downgraded McClure's later discovery of a passage

farther north. Unlike Franklin, McClure had actually traversed the passage from west to east, though not entirely by water. But Franklin was a popular favourite. Indeed, the eleven-year search for the lost ships elevated him to Arctic sainthood.

To the *New York Times* he was "one of the ablest, oldest, and bravest men who had trodden that perilous path." The paper praised the expedition and the search that followed as being "as noble an epic as that which has immortalized the fall of Troy, or the conquest of Jerusalem."

The *Times* wrote of "unheard-of fortitude," "religious heroism," "courageous endeavour," and "devotion to duty," in the face of "appalling perils" – phrases of the day that were always brought out whenever another adventurer went to his death, planting his country's flag in the far corners of the world.

And so for Franklin there would be a tablet at Greenwich, and a bust in Westminster Abbey, and a breathless fragment of poetry by Alfred Lord Tennyson, the poet laureate. No matter that the picture of the last days of the expedition, pieced together by M'Clintock, and later investigators, was bitterly ironic. For it is a picture of inadequately clothed, badly nourished men, dragging unmanageable loads down the bleak coast of an Arctic island.

As they stumble and drop in their tracks, other eyes watch them curiously. The Inuit of King William Island were also hungry, and there were times also when they too suffered from the scurvy and even froze to death. But they were never wiped out. Meagre though their diet had been that winter, it kept them alive and reduced the risks of disease.

Cold they certainly were, even in their superior seal skins. But they were hardened to cold and knew how to prepare for it. The Inuit survived; the whites died to the last man. "They perished gloriously," to quote one of the letters to the *Times*. That was the general attitude. But if they and their contemporaries had paid more attention to the native way of life, they need not have perished at all.

INDEX

Coming Soon

THE RAILWAY PATHFINDERS

A few short years after Confederation the Canadian government decided the best way to unite the country's scattered provinces and fill up the space in between was to build a railway to the Pacific Ocean.

It was a heady and expensive dream – not least because much of what is now Canada was unexplored and unmapped. In THE RAILWAY PATHFINDERS, the first instalment in the series *Canada Moves West,* Pierre Berton celebrates the courage and accomplishments of the explorer-surveyors who crossed muskeg, prairie, and mountain to prepare the way for the steel rails to come.